BOOKS BY E. L. DOCTOROW

NOVELS

Welcome to Hard Times
Big As Life
The Book of Daniel
Ragtime

PLAY

Drinks Before Dinner

Drinks
Before Dinner

Drinks
Before Dinner

A PLAY BY

E. L. Doctorow

RANDOM HOUSE
NEW YORK

Library of Congress Cataloging in Publication Data

Doctorow, E L 1931–
Drinks before dinner.
I. Title.
PS3554.03D7   812'.5'4   78-21794
ISBN 0-394-40092-5

Manufactured in the United States of America
9 8 7 6 5 4 3 2
First Edition

Acknowledgments

FOR THE ORIGINAL PRODUCTION OF *Drinks Before Dinner* I was fortunate to have the association of Mike Nichols, director, who agitated consistently for a clarity of language and event, and in numerous ways contributed to my understanding of the play; Christopher Plummer, who brought his prodigious skills to the role of Edgar, and afforded me many crucial insights from the performer's point of view; and Joe Papp, producer, who created an environment conducive to experimentation, and provided both support and criticism in generous amounts. To them and to all the members of the cast and crew, I am deeply indebted.

TO SAM COHN

Introduction

THIS PLAY ORIGINATED NOT IN AN IDEA OR A CHARACTER OR A story, but in a sense of heightened language, a way of talking. It was not until I had the sound of it in my ear that I thought about saying something. The language preceded the intention. It's possible that the voice the writer discovers may only be the hallucination of his own force of will; nevertheless, the process of making something up is best experienced as fortuitous, unplanned, exploratory. You write to find out what it is you're writing. Marcel Duchamp was once asked why he gave up painting. "Too much of it is filling in," he is reported to have said. The worker in any medium had best give it up if he finds himself only filling in what has been previously declared and completed in his mind, a creative *fait accompli*. Writers live in language, and their seriousness of purpose is not compromised nor their convictions threatened if they acknowledge that the subject of any given work may be a contingency of the song.

Now, this language of the play, this way of talking, derives from two very odd sources, the prose of Gertrude Stein and Mao Tse-tung. I read a quotation of Mao's one day from a speech he gave to his officers in the field sometime in the 1930s. And the rhetoric of it was startlingly like Stein. I think now it is probable that anything transliterated from the Chinese sounds like Gertrude Stein, but I was set off nevertheless. I reasoned that a style of language common to an American expatriate avant-gardiste who lived in Paris seventy years ago and the political leader of eight hundred million people was worth the writer's attention.

I didn't analyze this language but merely set out to see if I could do it. It is a frankly rhetorical mode that loves repetition, the rhythm of repetition, and at its best finds the unit of sense not in the clause or the sentence, but in the discursion. I have since detected a similar sound in the recorded lectures of Zen masters and in sections of the Old Testament. Once you hear it, it is all around. It's a spoken language, a flexible language with possibilities of irony and paradox that are as extended as any modernist could wish, but a simplicity to satisfy the most primitive narrative impulse. I quickly and easily wrote four or five thousand words and took the opportunity to deliver them aloud several times in public readings in different parts of the country. I gradually understood I had composed a monologue, that someone was speaking and that he had a lot on his mind. His point of view was so single-minded in fact, and his dissatisfactions so vast, that everything he said could be answered by someone stepping a little bit to one side or the other of where he stood.

I began to respond to his remarks with the remarks of others. They were soon engaged in dialogue, and to keep things clear I had to give them all names. The one who started everything, the malcontent, I gave the name Edgar. But they were all in the same universe, these people; they were defined by how they spoke, in this heightened language that seemed to ebb and flow and rise and break on itself. The leisure for such language seemed to me to go hand in hand with privilege, Chairman Mao notwithstanding. I had a sense of time that had been bought, accomplishment of the kind our society endorses. So I put them into a dinner party (the habitual means by which privileged people wait for the next day), I put drinks in their hands, and I wrote the play.

NOW, WHAT THIS ACCOUNT SAYS ABOUT MY DRAMATURGY MAY seem to betray a serious flaw of composition. If the sound came first, the words second, and the names third, do we not have here a defective understanding of what theatre is supposed to do? Apart from the fact that I find among playwrights I admire a tendency of all their characters to speak the same way, I suspect so. Especially if we are talking of the American theatre, in which the presentation of the psychologized ego is so central as to be an article of faith. And that is the point. The idea of character as we normally celebrate it on the American stage is what this play seems to question. I must here confess to a disposition for a theatre of language, in which the contemplation of this man's fate or that woman's is illuminated by poetry or philosophical paradox or rhetoric or wit. A theatre of ideas is what has always interested me, plays in which the holding of ideas or the arguing of ideas is a matter of life or death, and characters take the ideas they hold as seriously as survival. All of this is, dramatically speaking, un-American. What is clearly American is the theatre of pathos wherein a story is told about this man or that woman to reveal how sad his or her life is, or how triumphant, or how he or she does not realize fulfillment as a human being, or does realize it, or is trapped in his or her own illusions, or is liberated from them, or fails to learn to communicate love, or learns, or is morally defeated by ethnic or economic circumstances, or is not defeated. Comic or melodramatic, this is the theatre of domestic biography, and I contrast it to any other—classical, absurdist, metaphysical, epic—that avoids its bias of sociological realism.

This theatrical mode has been so exhausted by television and film that I'm astounded it is still thought by playwrights to be useful and interesting. Because presumptions of form tend to control presumptions of thought, even what is most basic—the solicitation of emotion from an audience—must be questioned if the emotion is no more, finally, than self-congratulatory. Having written this play and seen it through its first production, I understand Brecht's disavowal of standard theatrical emotion not only as an ideological decision but as a felt abhorrence for what is so cheaply and easily generated. Since the onslaught of television in the late forties, the dramatic mode has swept through all the media; everything is dramatized—news events, the weather, hamburgers. The responsiveness of the media, print or electronic, to every new idea or event or terror is so instantaneous that, as many people have pointed out, experience itself has lost its value, which is to say, life as an experience rather than as a postulate for dramatic statement has begun to disappear from our understanding. Every protest, rage, every critique, is absorbed by our dramatizing machinery and then reissued in appropriate form. The writer confronts not only moral hideousness but the globally efficient self-examination in dramatic terms of that hideousness. Where is wisdom? Everyone has faster hands than the artist. His devices and tricks of the trade have long since been appropriated not only by the media but by the disciplines of social science, whose case studies, personal-

ity typing and composite social portraiture are the industrialized forms of storytelling.

WHAT ARE THE PRESUMPTIONS OF THOUGHT DETERMINED BY
the formal presumptions of this play? As it happens, the
corruption of human identity is exactly the preoccupation of
the speaker or character (not to be coy) who sets off the
action, and whose point of view annoys, frightens and, if I'm
right, finally enlightens the others. This is Edgar, whose complaint is with the weak Self that loses its corporeality to the
customs and conventions and institutions of modern life. His
dissatisfaction is so immense that he pulls a gun and looks for
someone to blame.

But not only Edgar but all of the others too who join him
in dispute speak in terms of human numbers, in images of
replicating humanity, and of themselves not as individuals but
as members of larger classes, and for a good deal of the time,
but especially at the beginning of the play, their argument is
in the first and third person plural. And when Edgar pulls the
gun it turns out that he is crucially unattached to the act: it
is the situation that determines what he is doing, the others
define him as much as he defines himself, and his own inten-
tions are something he may learn only as they occur—not
before. The images of replicating humans are reflected onstage in this one person divided from his subconscious im-
pulses.

So my characters are formal expressions of the basic passion
of the play—an imitative fallacy perhaps, but only if you want
from the theatre what you're used to. They seem to be uni-
formly well-to-do and reasonably well educated, but they have
no domestic biographies to offer, no childhoods to remember,

no religion, no regional identification. Only two, Joel and Alan, are given professions. There are no blood relationships except for the parents Joel and Claudette and their two children, but even this is conceptualized as an arbitrary genetic circumstance. Deprived of virtually everything else, these characters can only have their being from their positions in the dialogue. After Edgar proposes that they not have the evening they expect to have, the sides are drawn. His wife Joan is his first antagonist. She is succeeded by Joel and Claudette, who defend the life and attitudes that allow them to give parties and live well. Joel is perhaps less resolute and more foolish than Claudette, and he lacks her bitter fatalism, but he is quite capable of being clever at Edgar's expense. In Act Two, Joel and Claudette are superseded as antagonists by Alan, whose capacity for disguising himself as a function of the argument, agreeing or disagreeing with Edgar as tactics demand, gradually betrays him to a cynicism that loses the sympathy of everyone else in the room. For it is Alan who torpedoes the one presumption not questioned by Edgar insofar as he believes in the idea of the end of the world—the theological hope of redemption, of the possibility of something more through suffering and universal purgation.

As for Andrea and Michael, I think of them as the ballast of the play, their weight shifting to one side or the other as the moment demands, Andrea because she is willing to discuss anything, consider anything, in the spirit of self-improvement, or to mediate as one always sensitive to the feelings of others, and Michael, more mysteriously, because he is observant, and curious and thoughtful. I think it is Michael who becomes the most thoroughgoing disciple of Edgar, but for purposes entirely his own.

Drinks Before Dinner DEALS IN GENERAL STATEMENTS ABOUT the most common circumstances of our lives, the numbers of us, the cars we drive, the television we watch, the cities we live in, our contraception and our armaments, and our underlying sense of apocalypse. None of these circumstances are visible onstage except as imagery makes them visible. Instead of a play in which specific biographees suffer experience that we enlarge upon to reflect our own, instead of a progression from the particular person to the thematic implication, we have a play already in the region of the implicatory when the curtain rises. That is why it is so offensive. It is a play turned inside out. It displays human beings not filled in with the colors and textures of their individual peculiarity, but delineated from the outlines provided by the things that shape them, their technology, their failing rituals and faltering institutions, their platitudinous ideas and common fears. They are invisible presences, these people, ghosts, shown only as a space in their surroundings. Like Wells's Invisible Man, they can be seen only when wrapped in bandages.

Since the character of Edgar carries the burden of the argument, he is the center of the play's offense. Edgar is insufferable. He insists upon talking about what everyone knows. He is not a criminal psychopath, nor is he a revolutionary—two suggestions the others come up with to explain his behavior. He is not a psychopath, because he is fully connected to the realities of his life and is more interested, I suspect, in dramatizing the issues that obsess him, or in sharing his passion, than in killing or taking revenge. (The culmination of his violence occurs only when Alan, a man of power, seems unwilling to accept the moral responsibilities of his office.) And he is not a radical, because he offers no analysis as to why things are as he finds them. He can feel, he can describe, but he cannot explain. What he is, truly, is a person suffering from acute moral revulsion; he is a moral hysteric who has reached the limits of his endurance.

In fact, he sports some of the more unfortunate characteristics of the ancient prophets. Prophets went about exaggerating everything that was wrong in their society and they warned what would happen if things didn't change. They made dramatic, symbolic gestures to get their ideas across to people who didn't want to hear them: Isaiah went out naked and Jeremiah wore a yoke around his neck. Edgar brandishes a gun, the device of a world perfecting itself for Armageddon, but as with his antecedents, to make people listen whether they would like to or not. Certainly it is an arrogant role to choose for oneself, and for his trouble Edgar suffers the expropriation of his faith in the idea of redemption and renewal. So the joke is on him.

Nevertheless, a community of perception has been formed. Condemned, renounced and alone—dinner about to be served.

I MUST WARN FUTURE DIRECTORS AND ACTORS OF THE PLAY that with a language frankly rhetorical and sometimes incantatory, with a playwright who prefers a hundred words to one gesture, with a text that neglects the ordinary benefits of characterization and the interaction of ordinarily characterized persons, in which the spectacle is static and the words tumultuous and relentless (in fact, that is the first image I had of a production—a storm of language contained by a minimum of gesture and movement), this play does not solicit conventional theatrical sentiment from its audience. It should not be hammered and twisted in order to do so. The actors should be discouraged from imagining histories for their characters or inventing relationships not indicated in the text. They should put on the words, as their costumes, and see what happens.

On the whole the production should be conceived in such a way as to keep the audience from thinking in practical terms and asking practical questions—as, for example, why nobody takes the gun away from Edgar. Perhaps the play should be thought of as spoken opera, with aria and recitative, the music being in the imagery, the action more grand than behavioral. The stage has to go through several metaphorical transformations, from a living room to a hijacked teritory to an earth in apocalypse, to an ark. It might manage this more easily if the production did not suggest everyday naturalism.

The director will find a very thin line separating the portrayal of Edgar as a menace, or as no threat at all. Either extreme is wrong. Edgar is threatening but must keep the audience's allegiance. The real suspense is to see how much diffuse complaint the artist can get away with before the occasion loses its power. The answer lies in each individual Edgar. There must be enough tension in the introduction of the gun and its display, but not enough to appall the audience. In the original production the gun was handled as an unfamiliar object, definitely not as John Wayne or Clint Eastwood would handle it. In this country, perhaps now in all countries, the difficulty of introducing a gun onstage is in making it somehow more than the class of guns in Westerns, detective thrillers, guns in films and TV programs. The audience's easy familiarity with the guns of popular culture must be stripped away—the sense of this gun must be of one introduced into their own living room.

Another recourse is to play the play as the comedy it is, not just at the beginning but all the way through: play against the melodrama of the piece, just touch the gun to the head and forgo the tensions of realistically threatening to blow someone's brains out right there onstage. But in any case, Edgar should never leer, gloat, sneer, swagger or mock or tease the others. He is not *macho*. He is someone who helplessly tells his truth, as visionaries do, without tact. Acting against the lines, as it were, he may advance on Alan almost as if commanded by logic, and with glee, the gun to the head an extension of the argument, not the ending of it.

A final note: I have no compunction in saying that the last line of the play seems deliverable by either Claudette or Edgar, depending on the director's point of view. The text here has Claudette speaking the last line. This would suggest the solace of shared perception, the acceptance of Edgar by the others of the party, the only consolation of his sacrifice. The variant, in which Edgar reads the last line (as was done in the original production), dispenses with this consolation, Edgar using the line to carry his despair to a form of sardonic illumination in which even the newly opened eyes of the others is seen to be useless. And now, you're going to say it, he tells Claudette, in effect, and everything will go on and everything I've done here tonight will have resulted in nothing, changed nothing, except that I have given my life for a small episode between drinks and dinner.

But I like the ending as printed. We're on the ark, after all, and have been for some time.

E. L. D.

Drinks Before Dinner was first presented by
Joseph Papp at the New York Shakespeare
Festival, the Public/Newman Theater in New
York City on November 22, 1978, with the
following cast:

EDGAR   Christopher Plummer
JOAN   Zohra Lampert
JOEL   Charles Kimbrough
CLAUDETTE   Barbara eda-Young
MICHAEL   James Naughton
ANDREA   Maria Tucci
GRACE   Virginia Vestoff
ALAN   Josef Sommer
BOY   John Kimbrough
GIRL   Carrie Horner
MAID/HOUSEKEEPER   Fiona Hale

Directed by Mike Nichols
Designed by Tony Walton
Lighting designed by Jennifer Tipton
Make-up designed by Way Bandy

CAST OF CHARACTERS

EDGAR, married to
JOAN
MICHAEL, married to
ANDREA
JOEL, married to
CLAUDETTE
GRACE
ALAN (the guest of honor)
BOY, aged ten, son of Joel and Claudette
GIRL, aged eight, daughter of Joel and Claudette
MAID/HOUSEKEEPER

Act One

The action takes place in the
modern, well-appointed sitting
room of a New York City
apartment. Big window upstage with a view
of the skyline at night.
Three couples are having drinks.
The couples are

EDGAR and JOAN
MICHAEL and ANDREA
JOEL and CLAUDETTE (the host and hostess)

also onstage are a maid/housekeeper and two
children

Later in this scene another guest, GRACE, will
join the party

SCENE 1

(*At curtain: the preliminary stage of a dinner party when the host and hostess,* JOEL *and* CLAUDETTE, *present their children to the guests. There are two children, a* BOY *and* GIRL, *ten and eight, in night clothes*).

EDGAR   I won't survive this evening.

JOAN   Don't be that way. They're lovely. Their parents are right to show them off.

(*The children are kissed by everyone and led off by the* MAID. *Drinks and hors d'oeuvres are served*)

EDGAR   Forgive me, but let's not have the evening we all expect to have. I won't survive it. The children are beautiful but we would say so even if they were not. It's one of the things we say. We all know what we say. We say of artists that we like them or that we don't like them. We say of servants that they are difficult. We say of the hors d'oeuvres that we are on a diet. We say of the market that it is depressed. We say of a couple splitting it's amazing it lasted as long as it did. And the hostess knows if her party is to be a success she must have someone of whom everyone has heard. And the guests form their opinions of the person of whom everyone has heard. And we all come away with a story for the next dinner party where we will all know what we say and meet someone of whom everyone has heard.

JOAN   And so, dear friends, adieu. It's been a lovely evening.

CLAUDETTE   But that barely begins to suggest the interest of
a dinner party. He assumes conversation is limited to what
is said. You haven't mentioned the subtle and engrossing
judgments we make of each other as we talk. The exquisite,
discreet flirtations with which we entertain one another as
we talk.

JOEL   And what about drinking? He's left that out too.

CLAUDETTE   You're a hard man, Edgar. Yes, someone is
coming to my party of whom everyone has heard. I'm
having someone the whole world knows! What am I to do?
I was looking forward to my evening. I thought it would
be memorable. What would you like it to be?

EDGAR   I don't know. Memorable. Yes, for God's sake, let it
be memorable. Because something peculiar is going on,
and I don't know what it is. Nothing interests me. The
things I've always done no longer seem worth doing. Whatever it was I believed is not worth believing. You're all
friends of enormous charm and glamour, but I can't believe
you still believe in the lives we lead. It's very odd. Everything seems to me as tiresome as everything else. Everyone
seems to be as foolish and as vain as everyone else. Nothing
seems to be unquestionably worth doing. We are bored by
everything and believe nothing, but we're all going along
on momentum, believing in what we did and believed in
before because we don't know what else to do.

JOAN   Edgar, if you were not feeling social, you should have
excused yourself from the evening. We should not have
come. That is the way to handle this sort of thing. There
are appropriate occasions for the expression of dark despair,
but this is not one of them.

EDGAR   I want to speak of something that matters. Why is
that unsocial? Because you're invited to dinner, must you
abandon your mind?

CLAUDETTE   Actually, I rather like this tack. I rather like it.

EDGAR   I'm sure I can't be the only one to feel this way. It
amazes me how little I have to do in order to survive. It's
astonishing what little investment of care or attention secures for me the right to live another day, and secures it
in some comfort. I have to wonder if others do as little as
I do. Do you care as little as I care? How has this happened?
How do we get away with it?

ANDREA   I recognize that feeling. I think secretly everyone
knows more than I know and is more competent in everything than I am. I feel if everyone knew how little I do, I
would be sent away. You know, as children are from games:
You can't play. I'm waiting to be told I can't play.

JOEL   Well, Andrea, I would never tell someone as lovely as
you that she couldn't play. And I don't share Edgar's malaise. I like what I do and I think it's useful. Doctors are
coming in for criticism these days, much of it justified.
We're not perfect. But I like what I do and I think I do
it well. I'm happy to be in a society that allows me to do
something useful, and to be paid well for doing it.

EDGAR   The point is, Joel, whose resources are maintaining
us, I with my malaise and you with your smug self-satisfac-
tion? Someone still has energy, but who? Not you. Not I.
I see in my friends' eyes feelings similar to my feelings. Is
it our age? We have no more lust for our wives and no more
attention for each other. We have no more lust for each
other's wives! We think of the young women who are
available to us as pockets of desire and ignorance, as repeti-

tions, we think of passion as repetition, and of passionate young women as repetitions of other passionate young women. Suppose someone were to walk in right now and I were immediately to fall in love. A little time sets everything right. If you smell the sweet hair of a young girl, it's the scent of her shampoo. Very soon there are small defections from the thrall of love. She is reading the morning newspaper before you're out the door. She says something about a failing or fault of yours, not in criticism, but as someone who occupies your flaw or failing as you yourself do. One evening you have an intense discussion about the future. She turns out to plan ahead, like your wife. One day you see they have separately bought the same dress. They have separately chosen the same scarf and separately want to know if you like it.

JOAN   I should explain that Edgar hasn't begun to speak frankly of his feelings and his lusts only now when they're obsolete; he has always broadcast the state of his feelings. He has always shared his feelings, whatever they were, with me as with his previous wives, and in fact has been generous enough to assign us a share of responsibility for those feelings. I notice now the young women to whom he is not married have come in for their share of responsibility. I find that interesting.

CLAUDETTE   Joel, perhaps someone wants another drink?

JOAN   But in Edgar's life of changing feelings one thing remains the same and it is that women are creatures upon whom he makes his choices. We may be wives or passionate young women repetitious of other passionate young women, but we are here for him to do with as he chooses, to be fucked or not to be fucked, because we exist solely for the sake of his choosing, so that he may resolve his changing definitions of himself and make his aesthetic distinctions, and carry on the progress of his moral life.

EDGAR   Maybe it is chauvinist to mourn the failure of love or the death of the presumption of love. But you seem capable, without any grant from me, of making your own moral distinctions and carrying on the progress of your own moral life. You don't need permission from me. Surely what women have been saying in the past few years is that marriage proves nothing and sustains no one. Why do you fight it? What small damp hankie of domestic hope do you carry balled in your fist? How many friends of yours were separated last week? How many divorced? We need a calculator to keep track of these things. Here is a husband with his vasectomy discovering the diaphragm in his wife's purse. Here is a wife turning off the downstairs lights at dawn. Here they are arguing about what one of them said to the other. Here they are arguing about how much one of them drinks. Or how much one of them spends. Or here they are arguing about nothing at all, talking about nothing at all, in no apparent conflict at all. Here she is running to the bank with the passbooks. Here he is shouting at his lawyer. Marriages are bombed, machine-gunned, they fall away screaming with their arms thrown up.

ANDREA   Oh, that is too frightening to talk about. It is true. And you always wonder when you are next, when your death of love is next, because the war is all around you.

EDGAR   We're all changing. None of us is exempt. It is happening to us all. How can I be a chauvinist if my personality no longer supports me, if it has failed, if my concept of the person has failed, if our reasons for the person are failing, and that all of us now in this country, fucking or being fucked, are persons whose being as persons has failed.

JOEL   Is that all it is? For a moment I thought it was serious.

CLAUDETTE   Tell me, Edgar, don't you enjoy anything? Is nothing right? Is nothing good? Doesn't anything give you pleasure? Perhaps these things you're saying give you pleasure, perhaps you like to distinguish yourself by saying these things. But to me it's like juggling or standing on your head —it's impressive and distinctive, but of no demonstrable importance.

EDGAR   But everyone knows what I'm saying. I can't distinguish myself by saying these things. We are all saying them. Our novelists in books, our crooners in Las Vegas, our social workers and church spokesmen, our killers in saloons and our maniacs in wards—who is not saying these things? We reward people who say these things in the right way. This is the culture of saying things, this is the society in which these things are supposed to be said. The very fact of our saying these things is part of what these things are. So what you see when you walk the streets are people rushing along like this with radios to their ears. They are listening to the radios as they walk. They watch television when they get home and turn on the record players while the television sets are going; they are trying to keep up. They are reading papers as they walk along listening to radios. They are stopping in front of appliance stores to watch the banks of TV sets while they listen to their radios with their newspapers tucked under their arms. They don't know how to keep up. They are reading reviews of movies based on plays taken from novels. They are going to school to study the novels upon which films they have seen are

based. They remember the films about the lives of the
authors of the novels they study upon which the lectures
are based. They are trying to keep up.

JOEL   Well, if I understand Edgar correctly, he's saying our
culture consumes us. But didn't people say that too in the
eighteenth century when novels began to be published? He
also says that passion does not last, but I am not sure it
should. Can you imagine the effect of a constant lifelong
passion on one's prostate? He says our relationships are
easily duplicated. But that's what it means to have been
evicted from Eden. So where's the news in any of this? It
has undoubtedly been true before our time that it appeared
to somebody or other that nothing seemed to be worth
doing. So it is tiresome to wring one's hands over this.
Perhaps something crucial has happened and we are
becoming depleted persons in some way. But I look around
and see so much unregenerate ego in human beings that
I would welcome a loss of person for all of us, across the
board. In fact, it is hugely funny to me that Edgar, with
his formidable ego and a mind given over to its own inimi-
table hysteria, should worry over his loss of character. It is
enormously funny. A doctor learns early in his career that
most illnesses are imaginary. It is a form of narcissism, of
course. People love themselves more in the fear of death.

ANDREA   But he is talking of how we are compromised, and
I understand that. I really understand that. The way we all
duplicate each other. I really do understand that and feel
that when I walk in the street and see other girls not only
wearing my clothes but walking my walk. Oh, how I understand that. Life is becoming unclear. The lines are disap-
pearing. I see women who are men and men who are

women. I suppose I should say my idea of life is no longer clear. I see in old movies dead people who are still alive. They live in states of high drama. They have more life than I have.

CLAUDETTE Good, Andrea dear. Let it be that way. Drama is to be avoided. I want to live my life as undramatically as possible. I want to live quietly and watch my children grow and keep my family fed and clean and enjoy beautiful things, and not be hurt by anyone. Besides which, whatever we know about our lives, we go on living them. Isn't that right? Even you, Andrea. Even Edgar. No matter what we say of it, life requires us to go on living it. It is the custom of life to go on with itself no matter what we say or what we feel. It has that aspect of requiring us to go on with it. Life is so totally careless of what we feel or what we know, or think we feel or think we know, that all our emotions and thoughts are continuously superseded by other emotions and other thoughts because life pushes on and forces us to continue living it. So that even if we are blissfully happy, it pushes on until we are not; even if we are in love, it pushes on until we are not; and even if we discover something marvelous or do something that makes us famous, it pushes on. It just goes through a whole lifetime of our feelings, careless of all of them, not giving a damn for any of them, except I suppose our last feeling before we die. When we have got life to stop to accommodate our feeling, we die. And what we said about it and felt about it is gone, and what we thought is gone, and our anger is gone, and the expression of our eyes and the character of our smiles, that's all gone. And if we knew how to embroider or sing "Bye Bye Blackbird," that's gone too.

JOEL   So it is clear, then, that those who do best in life are those who get on with it. Life is surely merciful to those who get on with it. Yes. So that is what we do. We get up in the morning and go about our business. We get up and go to our jobs, if we have jobs, or to the unemployment lines those who don't have them. And there is the holding of a job and then losing it, or the looking for a job and not finding it, and of course the getting of a job and hating it. All that is getting on with it. Meeting someone, making a marriage of whatever duration, is getting on with it. Having a job and having a family is surely getting on with it. And everyone each morning, no matter what his or her feelings, gets up and gets on with it. And that is what makes the romance of the cities.

MICHAEL   I beg your pardon, did you say the romance of the cities?

JOEL   Look at those lights. Isn't that romance? Isn't that human enterprise shining like a constellation? Don't tell me I can't walk in the park at night. We're a great civilization. There was poverty and disease in Renaissance Italy. There was filth and degradation in Edwardian London. Were these not great civilizations? You feel the romance of the city by living in it. You feel it in the lights of the evening, you feel it in the day when everyone is going about his business. A person's spirit is lifted by the doing of what everyone else is doing at the same time. That is the appeal, for example, of public dancing. That is the appeal of soldiers marching. In this country we work on our own behalf but together with others who work on their own behalf. The spirit is lifted by the numbers of people working for their future in the same rhythms as others working for their future. The spirit rises on the numbers of people going about their own business together through the streets in the mornings at random speeds and in different rhythms of walking.

EDGAR   Yes, so that the spirit is lifted that way, I can see that. It is lifted by the numbers of people walking to their places of business. I agree with that. It is lifted too by the numbers of derelicts marching through the streets to their places of business. It is lifted on the dancing steps of child prostitutes and in the happy song of their pimps. It is lifted on the merry tinkle of empty wine bottles breaking against the sides of buildings, it is lifted on the soaring coloratura of the police cars and ambulances and fire engines going about their business. And it's lifted to its heights in the exhalations of the dying. People who die, as they are murdered in the streets at night or in the operating rooms of the hospitals in the early morning, release with their last scream the great hallelujah of their dying, and altogether the stabbed and shot and butchered and starved, the overdosed and run-over and burned alive, lift the rest of our spirits in their chorus of dying breath so that we may gaze down in philosophic happiness at the greatness of our civilization.

(The sound of the doorbell. JOEL *and* CLAUDETTE *stand and look at each other)*

CLAUDETTE   But he said he'd be delayed. *(She goes to the doorway)* No, wait, it's Grace. Darling!

(Everyone regroups for the new arrival. GRACE *enters and is greeted by* CLAUDETTE, JOEL, *and then by* MICHAEL *and* ANDREA. EDGAR *and* JOAN *are, for a moment, alone)*

JOAN *(To* EDGAR)   What has gotten into you! Are you aware

of the pains they've taken to make this evening successful?
You're being awful! Putting everyone in a state, acting like
some nasty destructive child—if you don't stop, we'll be
asked to leave. In fact, I won't wait to be asked.

(The new guest, GRACE, *is led toward them and* JOAN *puts
on a smiling face.* CLAUDETTE's *introductions are not here
effusive. They are cursory first-name sort.* GRACE *sits down
and receives a drink. Almost everyone sits. There is an
awkward silence)*

GRACE   Has anyone seen the Hopper retrospective at the
Modern?

JOAN   Yes, isn't it marvelous?

GRACE   I was disappointed. I used to like Hopper. Now I find
I dislike him.

CLAUDETTE   Grace is a painter herself.

(EDGAR *makes an incoherent sound*)

GRACE   I beg your pardon?

JOEL   Perhaps you can help us, Grace. This evening Edgar
is in great pain. We're trying to console him, but he's
inconsolable. Today he went about his business as usual,
and tomorrow he will go about his usual business, but this
evening he finds himself inconsolable. Of course, by his
own admission he doesn't know anything the rest of us
don't know, nor perceive anything we can't perceive. We
all know and perceive the same things. As a physician I
probably have more of a reason than anyone to be inconsolable. I know of more disgusting and degrading means of
dying than anyone else in this room could possibly know.
Every day of the week I perform five or six operations of
the same kind. I get up early in the morning to do that.
Every day in the week thousands of physicians all over the

country get up very early in the morning to do the same operations for the people who have come to us for the same conditions for which other people have come to us. The admissions officers of hospital emergency rooms can calculate by the week and month and year how many knifings they will get, how many shootings, how many cardiac arrests, how many ODs, how many car wrecks. They know in advance. Cars go up on sidewalks, through store windows, they skid into each other in the rain, they collide at intersections, they crash head-on on the highways. It is very farcical what cars do. They run into lampposts or hurtle off bridges. Trains derail, buckle, plow into the rear of other trains. Airplanes take off and crash, and they crash on landing. They hit other airplanes in the air, they turn on their wingtips on the runway, they skid off the runway, they miss the runway altogether. Everything disastrous that happens to people usually happens to many people at the same time. They even get sick in great numbers, as in epidemics. You would think that illness was a personal thing and a matter of individual character, but people are poisoned in great numbers by the food they eat at the same dinners, or they get cancer together from working in the same factories. There is very little that people can do disastrously by themselves. Neither crashing in airplanes nor burning to death in tenements. Most of the time, these things are done by groups of people. And of course, war is done by groups of people, and the dying in wars is comprised of enormous numbers of people. In fact, that is the meaning of dying in wars, that it be done by the greatest possible numbers of people. So it is all very painful. There's very little dignity possible and I find that quite painful. Nevertheless, nevertheless, I choose not to be inconsolable.

GRACE   I am not sure why you are telling me this but I think you are wise not to be inconsolable.

(In the ensuing laughter EDGAR *distractedly takes a handgun from his breast pocket)*

EDGAR   Very wise. Very brave.

JOAN   What is that?

CLAUDETTE   Is that a gun?

JOAN   Where does that come from?

CLAUDETTE   Joel—

JOEL   It isn't loaded, I'm sure. Is it, Edgar? What is it, some sort of *objet?*

EDGAR   I don't know.

MICHAEL   You'll go to great lengths to win an argument.

EDGAR   On the contrary. I didn't know I was inconsolable until it was said. It is exactly true.

JOAN   Where did you get that thing?

EDGAR   I bought it. Very cheap. I didn't know why, it just appealed to me.

(A moment of silence. The others exchange glances)

EDGAR *(Ruminatively)*   I am inconsolable! Yet I don't claim not to take pleasure where I can. I don't claim pleasures are not possible or desirable because everything is so painful. For instance, on a beautiful day in the city people buy sandwiches and take them to the parks to eat, or they sit in one of the plazas off the streets, one of the raised plazas or parks of the banks and corporations. And they watch each other go by. That is a simple, undeniable pleasure available to everyone. It is a precise pleasure to eat one's lunch in contentment and stare at the girls and think about them as they go by. It is nice to see the sun shine through the thin skirt of a lovely girl. When the weather is warm she may wear such a flimsy dress that you can see the sun shining through it, so that it lights her thighs. And if the sun is really strong, you can through your half-closed eyes see it shining through her dress, so that you can see her entire body, and through the flesh of her so that you can see her bones, and even through her bones so that you can see the most opaque intimate part of her, her intrauterine device.

JOAN   What are you trying to do? Put it away, please. What is it you want? What is it you hope for? When will you relent?

(Pause)

ANDREA   But you remind me of a story of the street and it happened today. I was on Fifth Avenue and I saw a young man standing on a corner. Edgar, he was a poet selling his poems that he had written and printed himself on broadsheets. He was a poet standing on the corner along with the peddlars of leather belts and strings of beads and watercolors of lions and tigers, but he had no luck selling his wares because the people walking somehow walked too quickly to be able to read a poem and like it and make a decision to buy it as they might buy a belt or beads or a watercolor. Perhaps he could see, of the lightly dressed girls passing him and ignoring him, their intrauterine devices. But he noticed not only that the girls ignoring him but that everyone ignoring him, walking and strolling and carrying their lunch in paper bags to the park or the slightly raised plazas of banks and corporations, was moving faster than the automobile traffic in the street. In fact, the traffic wasn't moving at all. So this enterprising young man turned his back to the people walking on the sidewalk, and took his poems out into the street into the traffic jam, and he began to sell them to the people sitting behind their steering wheels not going anywhere. And, you know, he did quite well!

*(*EDGAR *smiles. At this moment the children are heard, giggling, just out of sight)*

EDGAR *(Playfully)* Do I hear those naughty children? Where could they be!

(Everyone looks toward the sound of the laughter)

Curtain

SCENE 2

(As before. But the two children, in their bathrobes, are onstage as well. EDGAR, *holding the gun, is totally absorbed in his thoughts)*

EDGAR Your poet knew something, Andrea. We have our life in cars. We eat our meals in cars, we pay our bills from cars, we hear the news of the world—so why not take our poetry sitting behind the wheels of our cars. In cars we have conversation not otherwise possible—conversation more intimate than what is permissible when, as now, people face each other. There is an intimacy of conversation in cars produced by the fact that we sit together but face in the same direction. We watch the road and see the state of mind of what we say imposed upon the road. We drive our cars down the interstate while our lives go on inside them. But this is not to say we cannot see things from cars. We become aware of other drivers in their most acute moments of personal expression. In our cars on the roads and in the streets we habitually interfere with each other, our wills clash, we are made aware of the endless numbers of wills like our own, the infinite number of equally powered antagonistic wills, and apparently I am the kind of driver who habitually creates in others acute moments of personal expression. These moments are quite interesting. You look in the rear-view mirror, although if you think about it, all mirrors are rear-view mirrors, but as I say, you

see there on this small field of vision an acute expression
of character on the part of the stranger in his car behind
you. And what he does as you slow for a turn without giving
signal is throw his arms up in a gesture of despair, lifting
his head and opening his mouth in what looks to be some
sort of howl. In a car we gather impressions of another
person's character from minimal information, but we make
our judgments nonetheless. I love the sleek and souped-up
car filled with boys and girls that tears by recklessly and cuts
you off with unerring scornful precision. That is character.
I have seen old men drive with great dignity in old cars,
wavering at slow speeds as the memory of their lives wavers.
And in city traffic in hot weather you may see from your
stalled lane the drivers sitting there without moving in the
opposite direction. In this situation there is some embar-
rassment, considerable close examination is possible, moments of communion or recognition for the idiocy or pre-
tense or unimportance of our lives. A sense of our mutual
victimization in the system of cars. We look frankly into
each other's windows. I notice a high proportion of women
doing city driving of this kind. Older women tend to sit at
the wheel in a kind of hunch that suggests permanent
deformation. Young women with sunglasses lying as fash-
ionpieces in the crown of their hair may appear to ignore
you but examine your fender, your trim, your aerial.
Women who drive tend to lose their attractiveness as
women to their driver's expressions. They are not primarily
women but primarily drivers. As for those cars with families, they appear to me as genetic traps. Cars with families
are particular contraptions for the entrapment of certain
similar beings with similar facial structures. That is what

they seem to me. The members of the genetically trapped family look out of the car with identical eyes and at the same instant, and all the miseries of biological relationship are arranged on their faces. If they are laughing and one of them has a brutish face they all have brutish faces. Different sizes of the same brutish face are laughing. So cars suggest to me the dreariness of biology, the predictability of the plan of mindless excess by which we reproduce ourselves. Sometimes the children you see in cars seem to understand this, they understand communication between cars is possible, they don't pretend it doesn't exist as adults do, they welcome it, they want it, and they wave at you from the backs of station wagons or the rear seats of sedans. At such moments you see the children calling for freedom of themselves from genetic entrapment. They wave and could as easily be your own children. You wave back. I always wave back at the freedom of small creatures who understand for a moment how we all long to be released from our genetic traps, who understand how arbitrary is our relationship to others with the same features, how we all know each other by waving from our windows, how by just as easy a set of arbitrary genetic circumstances we could all be each other.

(During this speech everyone else has drifted away from EDGAR, *and regrouped so that he is left isolated on one side of the room)*

CLAUDETTE   I wonder, with your sensitive feeling for children, if we shouldn't allow these children to return to bed. They are tired and should be asleep by now.

EDGAR   They don't look tired. They look rather interested. You always wave, don't you?

BOY Yes.

GIRL What kind of car do *you* have?

EDGAR A good question. I drive an obscure, not-quite-working foreign car to express alienation. There are only tens of thousands on the road.

JOEL It's true that we extend our persons in our cars. I fail to see why that is terrible. In any event, it is inevitable. Everything we make is modeled on ourselves. The common valve is a mechanization of the sphincter, household plumbing mimics the bowels, and cameras are mechanical eyes. Our computers take our minds for the model and produce thought outside of our bodies. Every technical human achievement redesigns the self, re-creates it, and projects it. How could it be otherwise?

EDGAR *(Laughing)* As the arm hurling a stone becomes—a gun.

(He swings his arm and points the gun toward the doorway. At the same moment the MAID *enters, stops in her tracks)*

JOAN Edgar, please, I find that frightening.

(Pause)

MICHAEL You said you bought that gun. Why?

EDGAR Well, that's the point, I don't know why. I bought it without planning to, I bought it with no thought for guns or weapons of any kind until the moment the opportunity was given to me to buy it. Children, where do you think I was when this gun was offered to me?

BOY In your car?

GIRL *(Simultaneously)* Your car!

EDGAR Exactly so. You are very fine children. I was sitting in my car. It was late at night, I was alone, I was waiting for the light to change at the intersection of Third Avenue and a Hundred and Twentieth Street. The street was quite empty and a wind was blowing sheets of newspaper across the avenue. The intersection was brightly lit by our modern anticrime amber streetlights. Every tenement and boarded-up store was lit in ghastly amber light. So that this whole ruined avenue was lit as for easier inspection and could be seen without shadow, without darkness, like the inside of an always lit prison cell. And then, standing at the driver's window of my car, without my having seen him arrive, was a boy not much older than you, a boy with his palm out and this gun resting on his palm with the handle toward me. He asked me if I wanted to buy it. I said "Yes!" He said, "Lay down twenty." I gave him a twenty-dollar bill and he dropped the gun in my hand and he was gone. And I had the gun.

JOEL   That is a most interesting story.

EDGAR   Yes, I think so. I don't know if it works, although it smells as if it does. There is a faintly acrid odor at the muzzle. I have been wondering for days why I felt compelled to say yes when it was offered to me. I've been carrying it around ever since. Perhaps you can help me understand this.

JOEL   What? But how can you expect us to help you understand anything. If you were holding a porcelain or a picture or a rare book, we might be disposed to be helpful. We would all sit around and wonder why you bought it and what it could possibly mean, and some of us would like it and others would not care for it, and we would give you all the attention you thought you needed but not more than we wanted to give. We could even do that with the gun if you put it down somewhere out of the way. But look at

you: you have it in your hand. That hardly encourages us
to be understanding and helpful.

EDGAR   But I now realize, as I hadn't since the night I
bought it, that it is meant to be held in the hand.

JOEL   All right, then let me hold it. I have a hand. I'll hold
it.

EDGAR   We should consider that. But isn't it the nature of
a gun to be held in a hand that is inconsolable? Guns
belong to the inconsolable. Therefore you are not really
trustworthy. It would not be true to the occasion for you
to hold this gun. If there is any truth or meaning to be
derived from the occasion, we would not find it by having
you hold the gun. The occasion would be defeated.
(Long silence)

JOAN   I think it is important for everyone in this room to
remain quite calm while Edgar explains to us what he is
trying to say. It may be a joke in poor taste for him to hold
a gun and say things in this way, and perhaps later we may
make him understand this. But everything seems to be fine
as we sit here with our drinks. This is a dinner party, after
all; we all know each other and respect each other and there
may be a constructive lesson for all of us in this, so let us
hear what he has to say.

EDGAR   Yes, do let us hear. But you may disagree with me
as vehemently as you wish. Disagree, argue, object—nothing, I assure you, will enrage me as much as a patronizing,
officious remark of my wife's.

MICHAEL   What do you mean by not defeating the occasion?
How do we go about ensuring that? The final form of the
occasion is not yet realized. Is that what you mean? That
the guest of honor is still to arrive?

EDGAR   We've been talking of matters of consequence and this is what has evolved. So my little arms deal wasn't a separate event. Surely that is clear. It was not a separate inexplicable event. It was the beginning of something. I can tell you I have never owned a gun before and it generates in me a kind of nervous pleasure. It interests me to be holding this gun and I find myself interested in my ideas as I hold it. I am not bored holding it. And peculiarly enough, I look at you all and wonder why you don't have guns, why we are not all holding guns. Isn't that weird—it seems to me so much more natural a picture if we were all holding guns. This apartment should be filled with them. They should be stuffed in drawers and falling out of the medicine cabinets in the bathrooms, they should be in the children's toy chests. If that is the feeling I have, perhaps we are meant to share what it is that is to happen from this gun. Only this evening did I feel moved to take it out of my pocket, so perhaps we are meant to share the occasion in some way. But if you isolate me because I am holding this gun, if you decide I am on the brink of madness, for example, or over the brink, that could be ruinous.

CLAUDETTE   But what else can we think? What else are we to think as you brandish that thing and insist that the children and the staff be brought in here, and you wave that thing around until they are!

EDGAR   That is your construction of what I did. I waved nothing. Your housekeeper came, I suppose, to consult with you and she has been too paralyzed to move since. Your children wanted to join us again. They are in the house and already implicated in whatever happens here. Shouldn't they have some say in the matter?

CLAUDETTE   Very well, will you permit them to leave? If they have a say, I have a say, and if I want them to leave and their father wants them to leave, if I should take them in hand and leave this apartment, will you stop us?
(Pause)

EDGAR   I have not heard them say they want to leave. But if that is your instinct, you should follow it, if it feels correct, and I will see then what is correct for me.
(CLAUDETTE struggles with the idea of attempting to leave with the children. She cannot do it)

EDGAR   Oh, what a shame. After all, Claudette, you invited me to dinner, you thought I was acceptable in your house, perhaps you thought I was amusing, perhaps you even had some affection for me. And now you have judged me to be not recognizably human. We must be careful. It is Joan's nature to interpret her husband to the world in the worst possible light. Do you really see this as something hostile or mentally unstable? Does everyone else agree? Do you, Andrea? Michael, you could not agree with that.

MICHAEL   Well, without question you're committing a hostile act. But since you're generally sensitive to the state of our culture and the way we live, I might make an argument for an ironically hostile act, one in which you are less personally involved than you appear to be, with some offhand, distant, almost political cruelty about it. You appear to have hijacked a living room.

EDGAR   Well, that's better! After all, what would my destiny be, what could any of us hope for if it turned out that I had only gone crazy.

JOAN   I cannot believe you would have come to this. But quite clearly, you have. Therefore there is something wrong with me. I am to blame. I thought there were limits to his dissatisfaction. I thought there were limits to his capacity for unhappiness. There are no limits.

EDGAR So what have I commandeered here? I think I might have chosen a room less trendy. White upholstered modules, lots of chrome and Lucite. A spot of color on the walls, a modest Léger, a dubious Mondrian. A view of the park. All very standard. All what they're doing this year.

GRACE I feel I must speak. It's bad enough to walk into a fine Fifth Avenue building with excellent security only to meet a gunman in the very apartment of my dear friends Joel and Claudette. But that he also feels free to malign their taste is inexcusable.

CLAUDETTE Grace dear—

EDGAR No, no, it's all right. Grace feels that a gunman should know his place. But I live in an apartment like this. We all have apartments with beautiful things and we all have summer homes at the seashore. We all have cars like each other's cars, we all have safe-deposit boxes and we all have lives indistinguishable from each other's lives. So what shall we do? We none of us know our place.

CLAUDETTE Then what is it you want from us? If we are so hopeless, what do you expect from us? If we are so lost, why do you stay among us? Why do you come here and terrorize us?

(One of the children comforts CLAUDETTE. JOEL, *in turn, calms her)*

JOEL Edgar, you claim to want us cooperatively to decide what is happening here. But the opinions of the person who holds the gun have, somehow, more amplification than the opinions of the rest of us. What shall we do about that? I would not want to call you a hypocrite. I would not want to suggest that it is an act of fraud for you to encourage us to determine altogether what is to happen.

CLAUDETTE   Yes, you didn't ask our permission to bring a gun here. We didn't share that decision. We didn't know you had it and we didn't agree that you should have it or agree that you should bring it into this house. Yet you came here with it. And you knew you were going to pull it.

EDGAR   No, I had no idea! In fact, I had almost forgotten I was carrying it until Joel perceived I was inconsolable. I am grateful to him for that. Perhaps it is wrong to expect you to share the feeling of inconsolability. Perhaps it exists because it cannot be shared!

(Silence)

ANDREA   I have a confession. I did not tell in my story of the poet selling his poems in the street that I bought several of them. That is because they were mostly very bad poems. Only one was good and that was a plagiarism of Walt Whitman. I think it is important to clear that up. That is part of the story too. It is important that we all know all of the story that any of us tells. I edited my story for the sake of romance. I wanted Edgar to find someone from the crowd who distinguished himself in his enterprise. But of course the truth is that in our country, where the practice of poetry pays so little, there are enormous numbers of poets. In our country, where the practice of poetry is thought to be impractical and eccentric, there are astronomical numbers of poets! And they are all standing on street corners selling their poems or standing in country roads and writing their poems. They are all standing looking at the ground under their feet or at the sky over their head and making up poems about what is on the ground and what is in the sky. We may be unaware of their great numbers because they are forced to live among us as we live among ourselves, as workers and people without work, as patients in hospitals, as betrayed lovers and born and dying persons, but not as poets. And that's the way they live too. There may be almost as many poets in our country as there are cars. They are manufactured somewhere, perhaps in the English departments of universities. And so they are everywhere. Every town in the United States has its poet, just as you always find a Chinese restaurant wherever you happen to be. I think if every Chinese restaurant in the country had a poet inside, you would see how many poets there are. In fact, most of the restaurants would have to have several poets inside. Some of the poets would have to cook and some of them would have to dine. Some of them would stand behind the glass case containing the lichee nuts. And as time went on, there would be more poets than the Chinese restaurants would know what to do with, and poets would be waiting on lines outside the doors and down the streets.

(In the last few moments of this speech ANDREA *begins to laugh. But it is the kind of laughter that turns almost immediately to tears)*

EDGAR But why are you crying?

ANDREA Because it is enough to make me cry but not enough to make me hold a gun.

EDGAR Oh, Andrea, don't ask me to put down this gun. I find my hand wants to hold it. Is it possible the body makes the decision and the mind only understands it subsequently? That's how reflexes work, after all. The body does something and the mind recognizes what it has done. Perhaps the mind is only the body announcing what it has already done. When it's born it cries to announce it was born. When it's older it kills and announces it was angry. Do you think, do any of you think I would hurt you, that I wouldn't destroy myself a thousand times before bringing harm to you or the children? But something has begun that has to be allowed to happen. So Andrea, if you must cry, I must hold the gun. I'll hold it for all of us.

(Pause)

MICHAEL   I remember years ago a man running on the beach, a middle-aged man running alone at low tide. He was the first one I ever noticed. The runners those days ran alone. They ran on the beaches, or they ran on the tracks behind the universities. Today there are so many runners that they go in packs. And they are dressed to run. They're dressed in shoes that have been manufactured for them and sweatsuits and shorts and headbands manufactured for them. They run in the city along the river and they run in the streets of the suburbs. They run along the edges of highways past the gas stations and fast-food places. They run along the highways to enlarge their lungs and breathing capacities, to make their hearts strong and muscles firm, but I don't know why, because the cars get the air first, they can't run past the cars, and what is making their lungs large and hearts strong is pure lead and carbon monoxide. Still, they run and there are more of them than ever. Not only white middle-aged men, but boys and girls and older people and black people and most of all women. A lot of the runners are women. They do not appear as women, they appear as runners. Even when they're attractive, they're attractive as runners rather than as women. But as I say, they are all running. And I wonder, What is it their bodies have decided that their minds have yet to announce? Perhaps it is their secret acceptance of the need to train for what is going to happen. Perhaps the runners training along all the roads of the country, training on the trails of our national parks and down the main streets of small towns and in parks in our cities and in traffic packs on the highways are the unconscious training of the nation for the terrible thing to come. When this terrible thing comes, our runners hope to outrun it. I see no other reason to run along the highways and breathe car exhaust. They are learning not only to have strong hearts and limbs and large lungs, they are learning the directions in which to run, they are learning the routes, it is very interesting. But of course, if you talk to runners, they all tell you how much better they feel since they began to run. They'll not admit to be training for the time that will come when it is time to get away from whatever it is that is coming. They will not admit it, perhaps because their minds do not yet know it. And each day their number increases because more and more people want to be ready for the time when there is nothing left but to run, when nothing else will avail but to run, and they do not want to be among those who cannot run or who falter and stumble and collapse from the attempt to run. They do not want that. They intend to be able to run. Their bodies are in training but their minds haven't made the announcement. When will they make the announcement? I have no idea why they haven't already made the announcement.

(The sound of the doorbell)

JOEL   There is our guest of honor.

(The little GIRL *cries out.* EDGAR *drops down on his knees before her)*

EDGAR   What? What is the matter? What do you think is going to happen?

GIRL   The end of the world!

Curtain

Act Two

(*A few minutes later. Everyone onstage, as in Act One. But the guest of honor,* ALAN, *sits tied to a straight-back chair.* EDGAR *holds the gun.*)

EDGAR Speaking for all of us, Mr. Secretary, I can't tell you how thrilled we are to meet you, to have you here among us, in this very room, and to have experienced the almost mystical moment of your arrival just as the idea came over us that the world is coming to an end. You can imagine how we look forward to the views on this subject of our greatest statesman.

ANDREA The idea of the end of the world seems logical to me. It is a perfectly reasonable possibility that the world will soon end. I think I am more frightened of the thought of my own death in the ordinary way while everyone else goes on living than that I will die because the world ends. I find I am even curious to know how it will happen.

EDGAR Perhaps it's already begun. Perhaps that is what I feel, the already-begun ending. Perhaps I can feel it with some trace in my being of the instinct that allows animals in a forest to anticipate a storm or sense a fire before it can be sensed. Is something wrong with me, Mr. Secretary, or is something happening that I am only responding to with some awakened perception? There may be nothing the matter with me except that I feel this. We have lived past what we used to be and still think we are, and anticipate with the laid-back ears of an animal some terrible holocaust of the world. Perhaps we are running in perception, perhaps we are becoming new beings in this perception.

ALAN   There is nothing new about pistols. People have been running around and firing them for a long time.

EDGAR   That's true. But if the world were really coming to an end, I mean if that is truly the situation we are in, then surely the carrying of this pistol is as unprecedented as that. The world has never ended before. Whatever we do, then, becomes as new as the ending of the world. The power, the terrible might or power released by the ending of the world, releases in us first a perception of its end, an anticipation of its end first in the most sensitive of us, the children, and then, in disguised ways, in the rest of us, who run or who find themselves with pistols in their hands. It is up to us to understand through the actions of our bodies the announcements that are being made. Just as we attempt to understand the disguised announcements of our dreams.

ALAN   How peculiar to hear that idea expressed. I will tell you of a dream of mine. I have this dream on a regular basis. There is some state of war. There is some sort of revolution and I hear the drumming of feet. It is night—the sky is lit by fire. Shadows of men run among the trees. Wrecked helicopters lie like giant insects on suburban lawns. I don't know if I'm with the state or with the revolution. A priest comes to my home and gives me for safekeeping a parcel wrapped in newspaper and tied with twine. He is on the run. I take him through the backyards, through the woods, to a bluff overlooking the highway leading to the city. The highway is filled with tanks and military trucks with their headlights on. They are not moving. Their engines make the ground tremble. I point the way for the priest and we say farewell. I race back home. And when I open the parcel I find he has given me for safekeeping Adolf Hitler's dinner jacket.

MICHAEL Why, that could be an end of the world, all right.

CLAUDETTE Michael, have you gone mad? Alan, this man has forced us to tie you to a chair and you tell him your dreams? The world is not ending! Nothing is happening except that he is holding a gun and terrifying us all and threatening our lives. Nothing is happening except that he has frightened my children to such a degree that they are in fear of the end of the world. How do you condone this? How do you speak to him; why do you listen to him? Why are we allowing ourselves to be humiliated this way? It is the utmost form of humiliation to begin thinking like him.

ALAN Please, Claudette. I am not unaware of the position I'm in. Think of this as a negotiation.

EDGAR But what is it we're negotiating? The end of the world? How can that be negotiated? What single human is so stupidly arrogant to put himself in that role?

ALAN All revolutionaries want to end the world as they know it.

EDGAR You think I'm a revolutionary?

ALAN If you are not a revolutionary, then you are a criminal psychopath. One can be both, of course, but I'm giving you the benefit of the doubt.

EDGAR Things happen so fast. Determinations are made so fast. In the back of my mind I have not ruled out the possibility that we may yet sit down to dinner.

ALAN I would give up that idea if I were you. You are holding a roomful of people at gunpoint. Including several women and two children. They are not likely to agree happily to sit down to dinner with you. You are not only holding a gun but constructing a dangerous rationale for holding it. You are saying that if the world is coming to an end, then the carrying of a pistol is somehow appropriate, although you do not yet know in what way. Do I represent your position correctly?

EDGAR   It is unprecedented for me to be carrying this gun. My buying it was a mysterious act. A child sold it to me. Another child perceives the ending of the world. We must learn what it is the children know.

ALAN   The danger in your thinking, of course, is that any action can be justified, no matter how mad or destructive it is, if the world is presumed to be ending. Even if, granting for a moment, the world is ending, there is no guarantee that each and every person's anticipation or perception is worthy or appropriate. If you and I act differently or in opposite ways, who is to say which of our actions is appropriate. The true response to the anticipated end of the world might be to get down on our knees together and pray. Besides which, the world may not be ending. And I may be doing more for the world and all its revolutionary possibilities in deciding it is not going to end than you are in deciding that it is.

JOEL   Yes, and let me remind you that this man, our oldest dearest friend, whom you have so brutally abused, is a recipient of the Nobel Prize for Peace.

EDGAR *(To* ALAN*)*   Yes, your argument could have validity if not for that. I might seriously consider it if you were not someone apart from the rest of us. But you're famous. Your hosts invited you here not only for their own honor but altruistically to give you a quiet evening away from your public life. You have a public life. You have received the

Nobel Prize for peace and you dream of inheriting Hitler's dinner jacket. You are one of those whom society appoints to embody its values for the rest of us. How, then, can you judge what is appropriate or inappropriate? You no longer know what it means to be human. You are disqualified.

GRACE That is an outrage.

EDGAR But I mean nothing personal. It is precisely the point that none of us any longer can mean anything personal. Let us assume we are all beginning to realize the world is coming to an end. Andrea, for instance, is quite ready to have the world end. She contemplates the oblivion of us all with a degree of curiosity. So do I. Is there some connection between that feeling and everything we know? Everything being done, all our institutions, all our customs, should be announcing something. And if not just Andrea and I but the masses of people have this crucial perception, and the children with the clearest, most crucial perception of all have this perception, then obviously the way we are living begins to make sense. For what other reason would we all permit ourselves to live and to feel as we live and feel except that we perceive our end? What other reason could we have for giving ourselves over to the industrialization of our being? Why else would we dispose of our humanity like an idiot smearing his own shit over cars and furniture and fashion clothing and art? I am no longer a person. I am no longer distinguishable from anyone else, nor is anyone distinguishable from me. My acquaintances are arbitrary. I can move as easily among strangers as among friends. I can just as easily know the people I don't know as the people I do know. I can go anywhere in the country and call people I don't know by their first names. My most personal tastes and preferences are predicted in market studies that compute my age and color and education and income. I am a function of other things. This is what it means today to be human. And we know that. As we fade in the conviction that we exist and our lives are important, as personhood begins to be given up by men in anticipation of their own oblivion, human character, like a precious resource, is allocated to fewer and fewer individuals. These are political figures and wealthy beautiful people, film stars and TV talk personalities. They hold the proxies for our humanity. The people in the gossip columns and magazines are the appointed human beings for the rest of us. They are designated people with a capital *P*. Is that not preparing very well for the end? At the same time we relinquish our value to ourselves, we can believe everything is as it has been and everything we have believed is still worth believing. In this way we move painlessly to the end. Celebrities become our trusted kin. They live in our television sets. They are more familiar to us than our own families. We are industrialized, like our refrigerators and our cars. We are indistinguishable in our affections from those in the next house. And in this manner we are led painlessly on to the end.

JOEL Only our friend Edgar could seriously suggest the world is coming to an end because we watch TV.

EDGAR It is funny that a machine is everywhere transfixing people by the billions. Inside the machine, momentous events are played out, the drama proceeds inexorably to its end. To be followed by another momentous event, another drama. To be followed endlessly by mindlessly momentous events and endless drama. And where we are, outside the machine looking in, there is no drama. There is no drama in our lives because our lives no longer lead to anything. Our crises prove nothing. Our conflicts simply repeat themselves and lead to themselves repeating. Anger is simply anger. Conflict is simply conflict. We are not elevated by it, nor do we learn from it, nor can we avoid repeating it. If our relationships break down, we renew them with others. There are no momentous events. We don't marry our true loves, we don't know who they are. If a person dies, he dies. If he dies heroically, who can care? If he dies needlessly, we feel no less sorry. People die needlessly in the thousands and millions. Nothing is done about that. We don't punish their killers. We don't assign responsibility for their deaths. That would be drama. People commit great crimes and we have them to dinner. Everything goes on as before.

ALAN   Except tonight, apparently.

JOAN   Yes, Edgar can be understood, I think, as a person always trying to regain the state of drama. He is really very old-fashioned, my Edgar.

ALAN   I wish, however, I did not have to be punished twice for the same thing. I wish your old-fashioned Edgar, if he is going to kill me, would do so without lecturing me first.

EDGAR   Are you not comfortable, Mr. Secretary? The idea of this is not to inflict physical abuse. It is a symbolic act in intention. The abuse is of your power and eminence. Since, in fact, it is your person tied to the chair, you may suffer some confusion.

ALAN   That must be it.

EDGAR   This apartment has been hijacked. It is by the rights conveyed from piracy an area of space no longer part of the nation. This apartment is a new territory, a region of light in which the truth of our situation is acknowledged. That is revolutionary!

(EDGAR *goes out on the balcony and looks down at the street*)

CLAUDETTE   Oh, Alan, I am so sorry. I am so terribly terribly sorry.

ALAN   Please, Claudette, you must not reproach yourself.

GRACE   I had been looking forward to meeting you, sir, under more civilized circumstances.

JOEL   I'm going to make a run for the phone.

MICHAEL   Don't do it.

(EDGAR *returns*)

EDGAR   The moon is out. The moon is lighting the lake in Central Park, and at the entrance to this building I can see it reflected in the shiny tops of two black cars. Why do you need two cars, Mr. Secretary?

ALAN   The second car carries my security.

CLAUDETTE   Oh, Alan—

ALAN   They wanted to come up here to look around, but I told them it wasn't necessary. The joke's on me. Actually, I've always been embarrassed by them. I sometimes have the impression I exist for their sake, and that rather than doing me a service they derive tremendous and enviable satisfaction from a sense of the necessity of guarding me. I feel I am their illusion, and that I must pretend to be important and valuable to sustain it. That is why it is interesting to find a fellow like you echoing my most private feelings. You are obsessed with numbers: Consider someone in my position for whom the smallest comprehensible unit of concern is the nation. How do you think I feel? How can one maintain one's sense of self making decisions presumably on behalf of two hundred and fifty-odd million people? I have always felt my own character to be a fictional creation. It is quite arbitrary that I am who I am, doing what I do. I derive no personal satisfaction at all. What amazes me about finding myself sitting tied up in this chair and facing your handgun is why it has taken this long to happen. I regard it as a kindness of fate that I'm permitted to undergo this experience among dear old friends. It is people like Joel and Claudette who are my real security. They recall to me who I was when we all believed in our selfhood. I come back to them like a patient for an injection.

EDGAR What a charming and sympathetic man. How dangerous. You hear behind his charming and sympathetic voice the computer clicks of missiles calculating their trajectory.

ALAN The system you describe by which we accommodate our perception of the world's end is, however, an imperfect system. Look at the other side of the world to be destroyed. Have you ever been to China? There are eight hundred million people in China. The peasants march in step to their work in the fields. No one in China is alone. No one in China has ever been alone. One doesn't live alone, or travel alone, or think of oneself alone or think of oneself as an individual competing with others, or present oneself to others to the disadvantage of others. None of that is done. The children's blocks in China are made too heavy for one child. The self in China is too heavy for one person. The person in China can only be lifted by China. I should say they are much further along in their preparation for the end of the world than we are. They march in step painlessly to the end. Over here we're still protesting. We're still in the thrall of our expectations. We have these stray romantics and malcontents like yourself, stubbornly clinging to the pitiful ideals of humanism and doing foolish things.

EDGAR Ahh. You do believe the world is ending. I thought you might.

ALAN Well, after all, it's the only reasonable position to take.

(Pause)

MICHAEL Just a moment, Mr. Secretary. I wonder if you appreciate how disturbing it is to hear that view from someone in your position.

ALAN Oh, I quite appreciate it. I'm used to having people give weight to what I say. But why should this surprise you? If you're beginning to perceive the truth, hearing it from children, surely you must realize I would have known it for some time. Of course this is all off the record.

ANDREA I feel a chill. As Edgar proposed the world's end I thought I had the courage to meet it. Now I'm not sure. Why is that?

ALAN Perhaps the idea had a certain chic? Perhaps that has worn off.

ANDREA I beg your pardon, Mr. Secretary, but that's not it. Somehow your words are ruining the end of the world for me! I supposed the idea of ending the world contained the idea of replacing it with something better. But I don't get that feeling from you. I get the feeling of the dead end from you. I hope you will forgive my saying so.

ALAN You give me too much credit. I didn't make the world. I'm merely of it—like you, like everyone in this room. As individuals we are pitiful, as groups we're inhuman. That is our anguish, our cross. Nobody can do anything about that.

MICHAEL   Sir, I don't wish to appear rude or contentious, given the position you're in. But please reconsider what you're saying. If as individuals we're pitiful and as groups we're inhuman, if our mind can't find a place for itself—neither as something separate in each of us, nor something altogether in all of us—why, that truly portends the end of the world and we were finished before we began!

ALAN   So it appears.

MICHAEL   But can you say that? I mean, Edgar here sustains hope! All his despair for the way things are assumes there is something more. Everything he says expresses a longing for something more. Don't you, in your position, have the responsibility to want more—more than anyone?

ALAN   I'm sorry to disappoint you. If it is possible to save the world from ending in nuclear disaster, which I doubt, or from any of the ice-age things we may be bringing about, it will end some other way. It is inevitable. It will end by simply going on as it is and irresolutely turning past the point when it can be what it is and still continue. Our destructiveness is not specific. We are suicidal in the fullness of our being. The world will therefore end from the fullness of our creation of it. It is already ending in every possible way in which it can end. It is ending in all directions. Whatever we do inevitably brings it closer to its ending because everything around us which we have made for ourselves expresses the idea of its ending. It will end of the failure of the human mind to locate itself in any category it can imagine. It will end of the failure of human beings to be sufficiently human. If your friend has reason to find hope from that, then he is a fool.

EDGAR   Children—there is the answer! Look, look how this gun pulls me forward. It moves, it is magnetized! This was the reason it was given me, to hold it, homing in along the last few irresistible inches of its momentous journey.

CLAUDETTE   Oh God in heaven—

EDGAR   Think, Claudette, of the enormous distance it has come! From the street to your dinner party. We make death. We make death. In the fullness of our being we design it and engineer it and mine it and cast it and build it and assemble it and test it and aim it and make careers in it.

JOAN   For God's sake, Edgar! Somebody stop him!

EDGAR   This is nothing personal. It can't be stopped. It's the world coming to an end. Not brain matter but an arms cache will explode when I fire. This small shot will fuse the armament of the earth. Think of all the handguns, rifles, machine guns, grenades, torpedoes, shells, mines, fire-bombs, frag bombs, ground-to-ground missiles, ground-to-air missiles, heat-sensing bombs, self-propelling smart bombs, proton bombs, neutron bombs, nuclear warheads, multiple nuclear warheads—in this head. This warhead. It is plated in steel and rooted in concrete. This head is the world's unholy armory waiting to be lit by my tinder.

ANDREA   Edgar, it's not right! I dissociate myself from this!

EDGAR   A child gave it to me to end the world!

(He points the gun at ALAN's *head)*

MICHAEL   Edgar, wait!

EDGAR   Why should we wait? Why should we want to wait?

One shot will take it all out. Let's get to it. Let's get on with it! Let's see what's on the other side.

MICHAEL But he's lying! He knows something he's not telling us! Why should he believe in the end of the world? He has no right to believe in the end of the world! What does he know that he's not telling us? Are there plans? They have them for everything—wouldn't they have to have planned for the end of the world?

(EDGAR lowers the gun)

EDGAR Give him some whiskey someone. He's trembling.

(JOEL does this. He crouches next to ALAN and holds the glass)

ALAN Either shoot me or let me go. I know of no plan. If it exists, I know nothing about it.

MICHAEL It could exist. Edgar, it has to exist! And if it does, that is not quite the end of the world, is it? Something would go on, something would be left! He knows! If the government had to plan for the end of the world, what would they think of? What would they try to do?

(CLAUDETTE pulls her children close to her, kneels between them)

CLAUDETTE Children. They would try to save children. They would hope to save a few children.

JOEL Is that it, Alan? They would do that even if there was no hope, wouldn't they?

ANDREA Think, Mr. Secretary! Who would be called upon for the sake of the children!

ALAN They would not have to be called upon. They would respond on their own. There would be no plan. They would react instinctively . . . People who come into their own under states of extreme disaster . . . People who become

very interested and efficient in the teeth of disaster . . . Not
your sort . . . Not people who go to dinner parties. Unfash-
ionable people. You'd be bored by their conversation. But
they know things. They know how to survive. It would be
some instinctive effort of these people who would have the
brutal, insensitive strength to survive. It would be a conspiracy of survivors who would save the children. They
would attempt to save their own children, but if their
children didn't come up to the mark, they would find other
children.

(Pause)

EDGAR Go on.

ALAN They would make some astounding selfless effort of
organization to save some children. There would be help
from the government, but it would be secret and unofficial.
Officially the world would not be ending. Rockets and
space launches would be under heavy guard in various
places in the country. These would be for the purpose of
venting the torment of the masses who, despite all assur-
ances, would know that the world *was* ending. There would
be nothing painless about it. Enormous mobs of tor-
mented, mourning, enraged masses would periodically rush
the heavily guarded gantries of rockets officially denied to
be for the launching of survivors into space. They would
be massacred. An ethic of genocide will justify the killing
of these enraged masses. It will be seen as a form of mercy
to save people the experience of the world's end. And of
course the rockets and space launches will be dummies.
The space vehicles will be dummies. The conspiracy of
survivors will have decided that nature is not secure in
space, that life is not natural in space. They will have

designed something for the earth, some completely self sustaining ecosystem, a terrarium deep in the sea, perhaps, where the selected specimens of humanity can begin again. Yes. This would be a venture of scientists and military men with government technology at their disposal. Revolutionary groups protesting its elitism would try to sabotage it. Morally they would be right, but they would fail. Millions would die in protest. But our computers would secretly be scanning the traits of every child in the country just reaching breeding age. And at the moment the ecosystem was ready, the moment the ark was complete, the computers would designate the children who were to survive. All the weak and deformed would be eliminated, of course, all the congenitally deformed children with twisted spines or macrocephalic heads or arms attached to their shoulders. All the physically normal but ordinary, sensitive children would be eliminated too. Only champions would be chosen, champions of survival, champions of selfishness, cunning, muscular strength, sexual vigor, children with the ability to kill, and a complete lack of concern for the horrors of their own consciousness. Helicopters will come out of the night and land in the streets and on lawns and kidnap these children designated for survival. And while the world erupts, on some back road somewhere an ordinary yellow school bus will make its way unremarked and ignored through the chaos. In the yellow school bus will be the chosen children. Not many. Perhaps ten of them. Perhaps twenty or thirty. And the bus will turn a corner somewhere, in some mining town somewhere on a river. The light in the sky will be amber, and the old school bus will have turned in that light a darkened yellow, like an egg yolk. And it will go around a corner and be gone, and a few hours or days after it has disappeared, the last unprotected person on earth will be dead. The conspiracy of survivors will be dead. But the ark will be under way.

MICHAEL   My God.

ALAN   It's more than a plan, it's an inevitability. The same flaw in the human race that destroys it provides the conspiracy of survivors with the responses that save it. The same insufficient humanity that brings doom provides a few people with the insensitive strength to plan beyond the doom.

EDGAR   Yes. And we survive the fire as we survived the flood. Clouds of radiant poison will fall through the trees on the mountaintops and drift down the mountainsides into valleys. And while men in the night drum the earth with their running feet and people run in terror over the corpses of the deformed and mobs tear down the gantries of empty rockets and while people choke on their blackened tongues and cattle go down on their knees and cities explode and the seas boil—the children on the school bus will see this. They will have the vision of the world's end imprinted on their brains. And in numbers of generations and individuals to come, those memories will erupt at night in terrible dreams. And one day again in the universe these dreams will come true. The dreams will again come true because the children of the survivors will be made in their image and will build a new earth with the genius of the conspiracy of survival. Everything that has happened will happen again. The ark will be built to resemble a lavish apartment overlooking a ruined city. The ark will look like this room. We are on the ark now. The world has already ended.

(EDGAR unties ALAN. He points the gun at the floor and squeezes the trigger. Click)

ANDREA It wasn't loaded!

EDGAR No.

ANDREA You were never going to shoot anyone.

EDGAR *(Pausing)* No.

(ALAN rises from his chair, arranges his tie, his vest, buttons his jacket, shoots his cuffs. Recovers his eyeglasses from the coffee table)

ALAN You led me to believe I was at the point of death. What do you think you accomplished?

EDGAR Nothing. I accomplished nothing. You were already dead. I was looking into the eyes of a ghost born of ghosts. I heard it speaking the words of life. Maybe that's something. At least I know who I am.

ALAN I could have told you who you are. I've known from the beginning who you are. You're one of the beneficiaries of a society that has provided more to its own than any other in the history of civilization. You're one of those useless beneficiaries who is given everything but respects nothing—one of those hypocrites of privilege who condemns everything but relinquishes nothing. You are a whining, pulullating psychopath. You are one of the wretches of ingratitude who has risen to the top as scum rises to the top. You are scum. You're a hero of the precious sensibility whose genius is to say in a thousand clever ways how humanity disappoints you, but who if left to yourself would not survive a day. You wouldn't be able to feed yourself or clothe yourself or keep yourself warm. You wouldn't even know how to wipe your ass. You are one of those traitorous malcontents, one of those spiritual vandals who would like to be a revolutionary but hasn't the balls of a flea.

(He takes the gun from EDGAR*'s hand)*

EDGAR   God bless our class.

ALAN   It will give me great pleasure to decide what you deserve for this little entertainment. Yes, I will think of something. It will have all the trappings of justice that we've come to expect. But it will be well conceived, I can assure you. *(He walks to the doorway, stands and looks at them all)* I'll know I can reach you through your friends here. I hold you all responsible! To think the work I do protects and preserves your treacherous souls. *(To the* MAID*)* May I have my coat, please?

*(*ALAN *exits, followed by the* MAID. *There is a long silence. The* MAID *returns.* CLAUDETTE *goes to her, comforts her)*

CLAUDETTE   *(Looking toward the door)* Very well. *(Looking around the room)* Very well! First these children must go to bed. *(To the children)* Say good night to everyone. Go on.

(The children proceed to be kissed and hugged by everyone. This is done solemnly or fervently but in silence. JOAN *weeps. The children linger for an extra moment beside* EDGAR. *Then they are hugged tightly by* CLAUDETTE *and exit with* JOEL *and the* MAID*)*

EDGAR   So. It's turned out to be not a bad evening, after all.

JOAN   Even memorable.

CLAUDETTE   And now we'll go in to dinner.

Curtain

ABOUT THE AUTHOR

E. L. Doctorow was born in New York and
educated at Kenyon College and Columbia University.
His novels include *Welcome to Hard Times; The
Book of Daniel*, a National Book Award nominee; and
Ragtime, winner of the National Book Critics Circle
Award for fiction. *Drinks Before Dinner* was first
performed at the New York Shakespeare Festival's
Public Theater in the fall of 1978.